CHILDREN'S FAVORITE
MOVIE SONGS

ISBN 978-0-634-04149-5

HAL•LEONARD®
CORPORATION

7777 W. BLUEMOUND RD. P.O. BOX 13819 MILWAUKEE, WI 53213

Visit Hal Leonard Online at
www.halleonard.com

PREFACE

The songs we hear at the movies find a special place in our memories. "Do-Re-Mi" is the first song I remember hearing in the movie theatre. It was such an exciting experience that, to this day, I can recall the unique flavor of that magical afternoon. My daughter, Lindsay, had the same rich experience with "Beauty and the Beast"...some twenty-five years later. She will cherish the moment and the song always.

Children, like adults, know a good song when they hear it. The songs in this collection are definite favorites of kids everywhere.

See you at the movies!

Phillip Keveren

◆

BIOGRAPHY

Phillip Keveren, a multi-talented keyboard artist and composer, has composed original works in a variety of genres from piano solo to symphonic orchestra. Mr. Keveren gives frequent concerts and workshops for teachers and their students in the United States, Canada, Europe, and Asia. Mr. Keveren holds a B.M. in composition from California State University Northridge and a M.M. in composition from the University of Southern California.

CONTENTS

THE BARE NECESSITIES
from Walt Disney's THE JUNGLE BOOK

Words and Music by TERRY GILKYSON
Arranged by Phillip Keveren

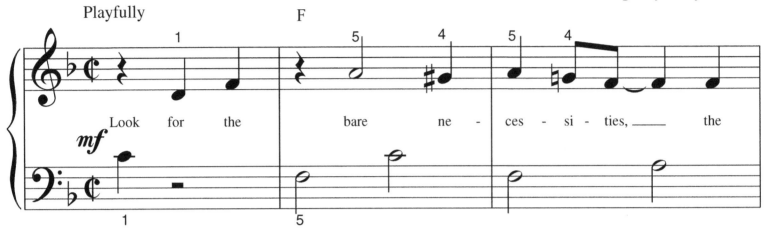

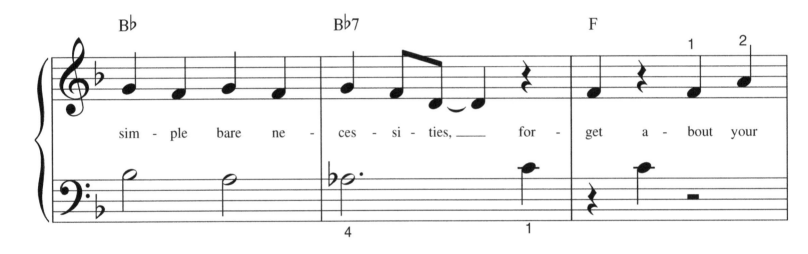

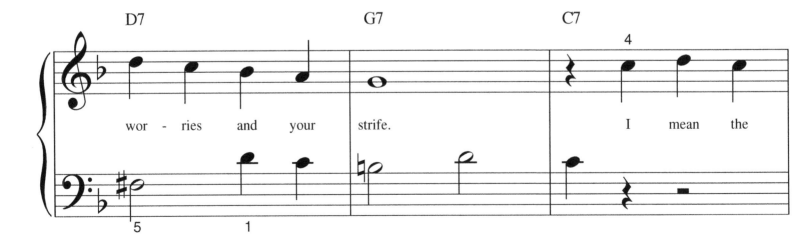

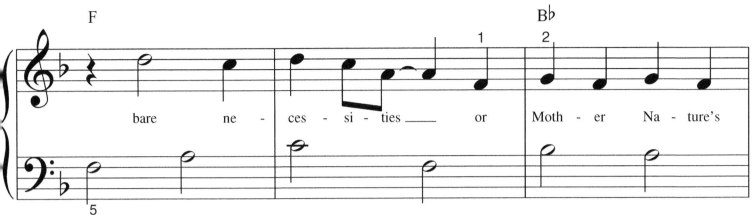

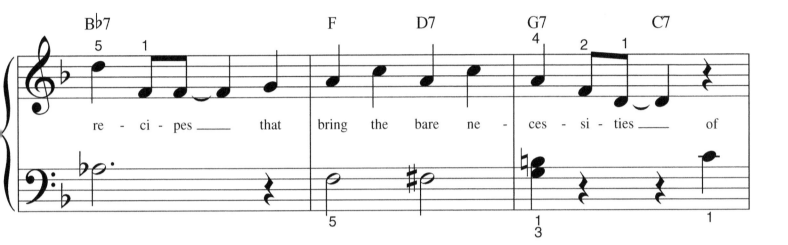

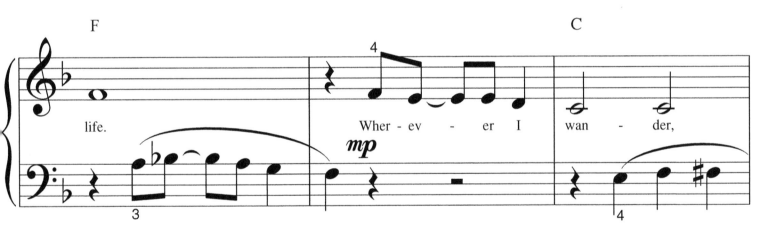

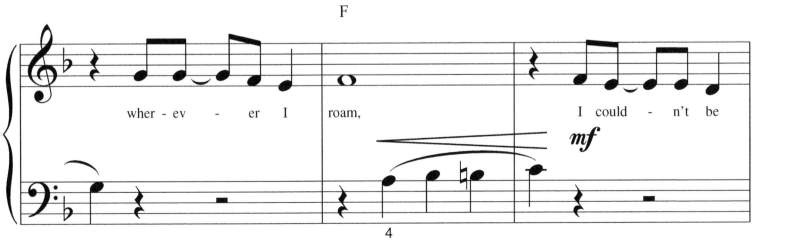

fond - er   of my big   home.

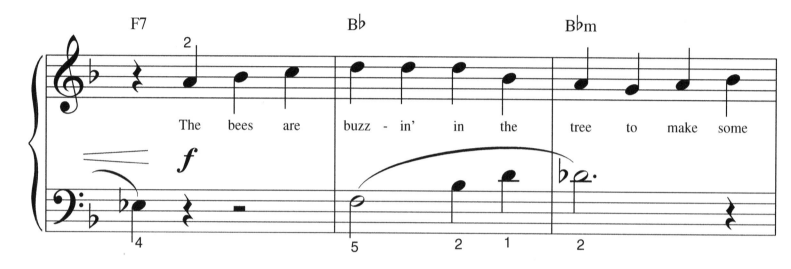

The bees are   buzz - in' in the   tree to make some

hon - ey just for   me. The bare ne -   ces - si - ties   of

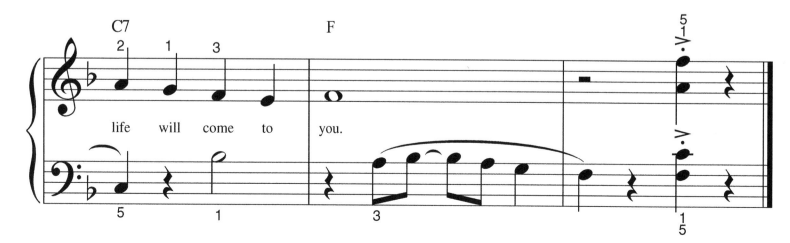

life will come to   you.

Can You Feel THE LOVE TONIGHT

from Walt Disney Pictures' THE LION KING

Music by ELTON JOHN
Lyrics by TIM RICE
Arranged by Phillip Keveren

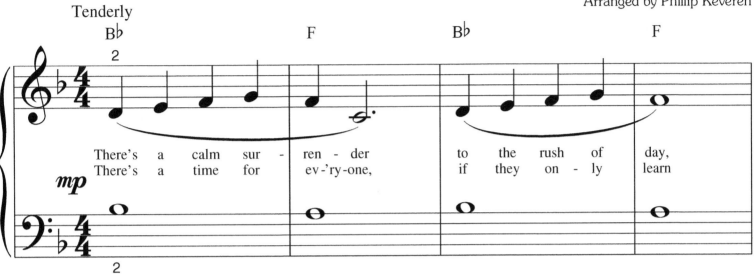

There's a calm sur - ren - der to the rush of day,
There's a time for ev - 'ry-one, if they on - ly learn

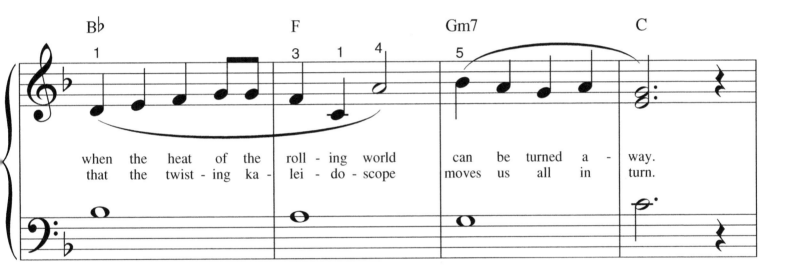

when the heat of the roll - ing world can be turned a - way.
that the twist - ing ka - lei - do - scope moves us all in turn.

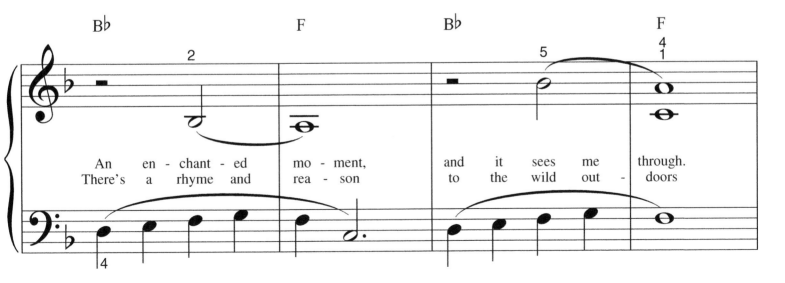

An en - chant - ed mo - ment, and it sees me through.
There's a rhyme and rea - son to the wild out - doors

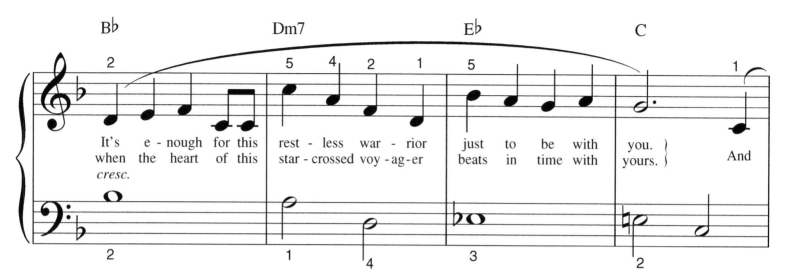

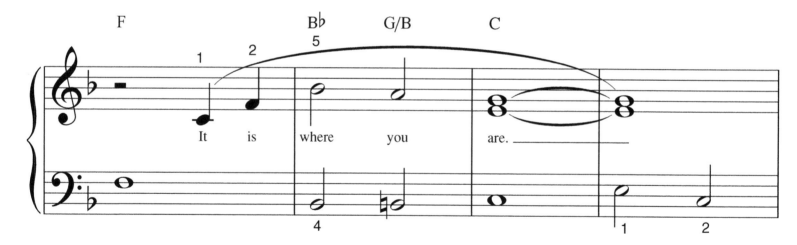

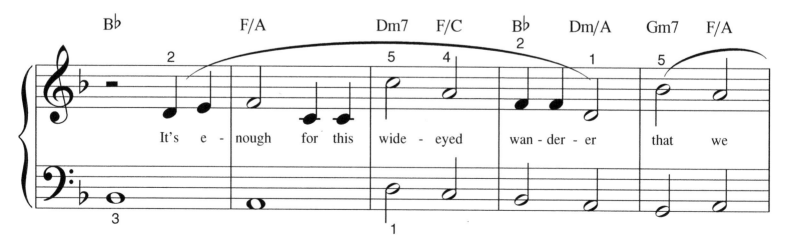

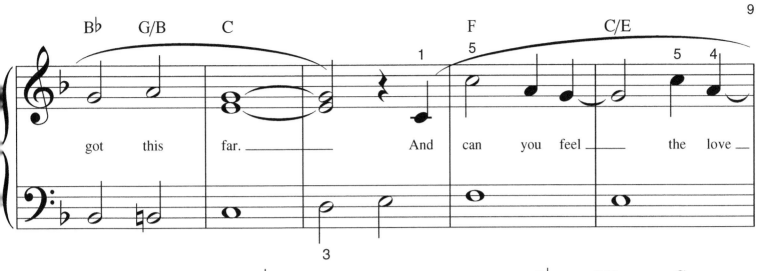

got this far. _____ And can you feel ___ the love ___

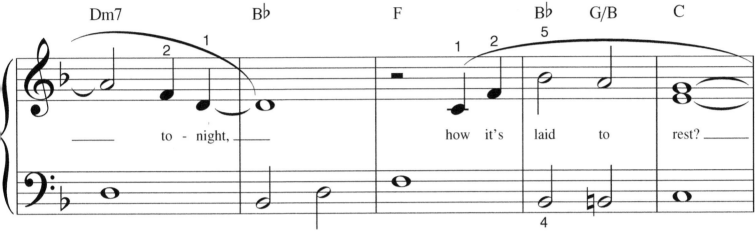

___ to - night, ___ how it's laid to rest? ___

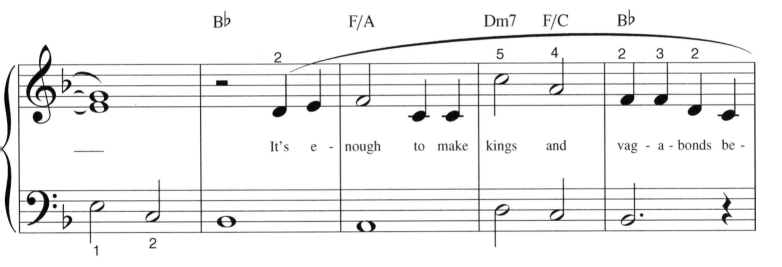

___ It's e - nough to make kings and vag - a - bonds be -

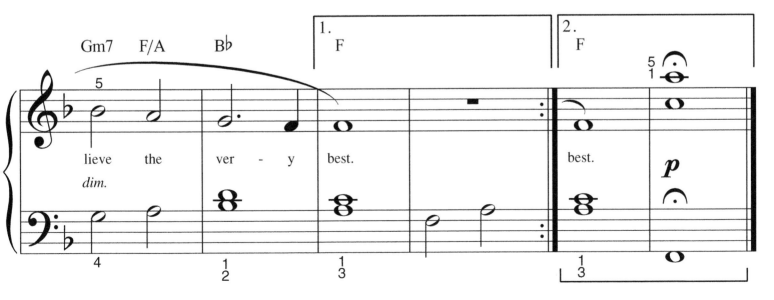

lieve the ver - y best. best.

dim.

p

BEAUTY AND THE BEAST
from Walt Disney's BEAUTY AND THE BEAST

Lyrics by HOWARD ASHMAN
Music by ALAN MENKEN
Arranged by Phillip Keveren

DO-RE-MI
from THE SOUND OF MUSIC

Lyrics by OSCAR HAMMERSTEIN II
Music by RICHARD RODGERS
Arranged by Phillip Keveren

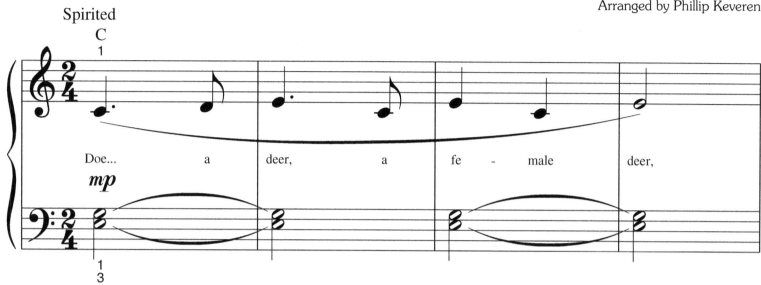

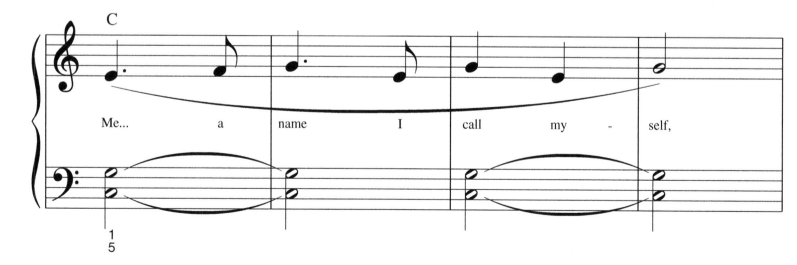

13

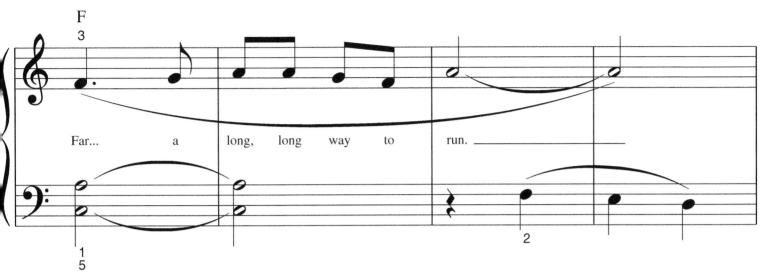

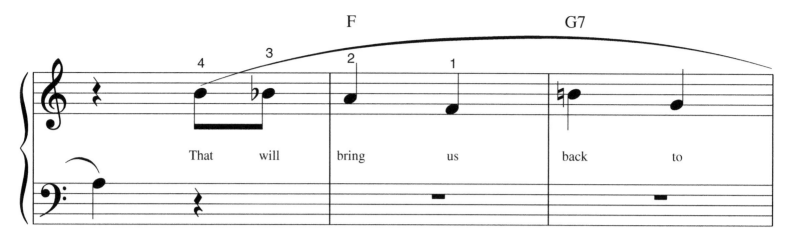

That will bring us back to

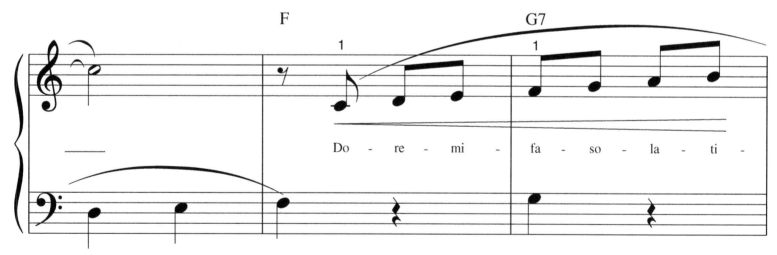

do - oh - oh - oh! doe!

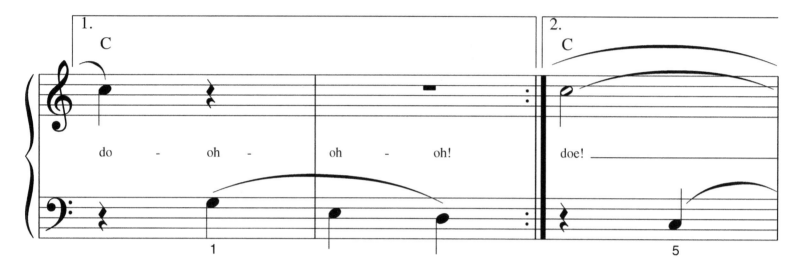

Do - re - mi - fa - so - la - ti -

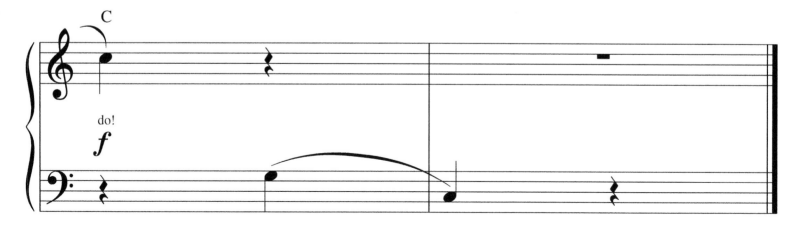

do!

FEED THE BIRDS
from Walt Disney's MARY POPPINS

Words and Music by RICHARD M. SHERMAN
and ROBERT B. SHERMAN
Arranged by Phillip Keveren

Slowly

16

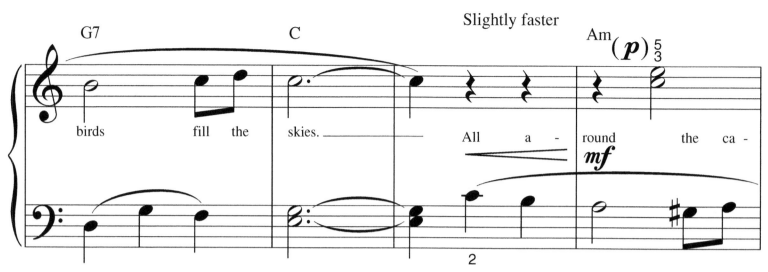

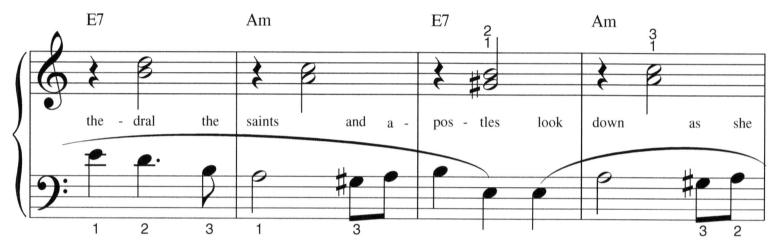

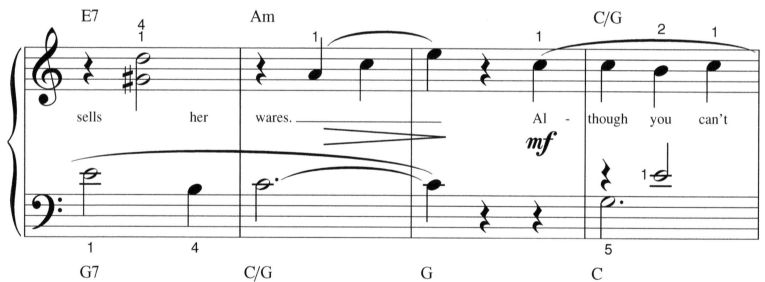

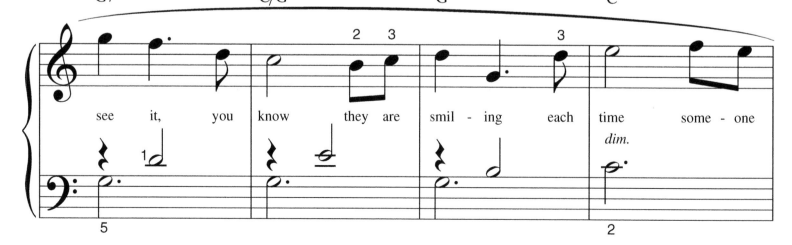

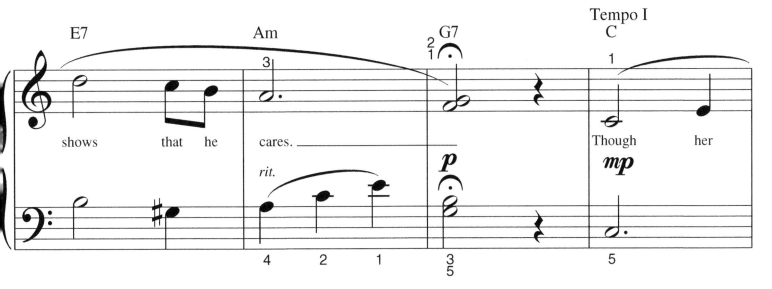

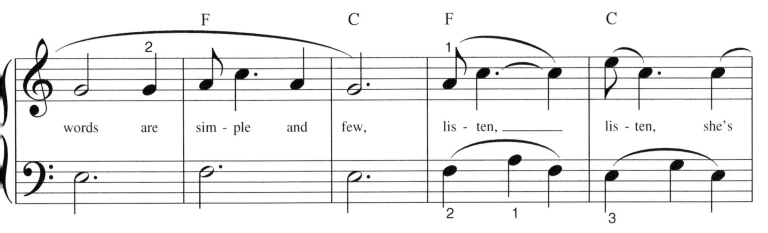

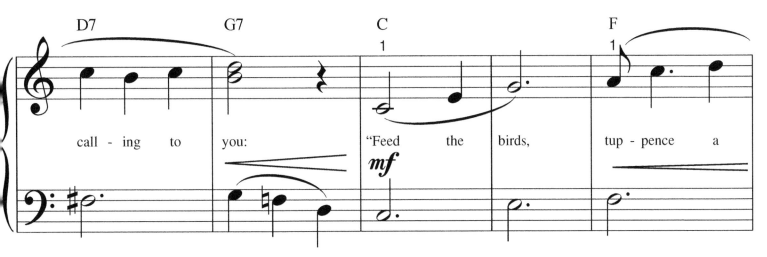

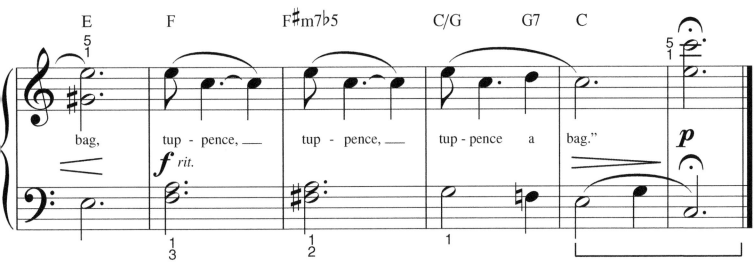

IN MY OWN LITTLE CORNER

from CINDERELLA

Lyrics by OSCAR HAMMERSTEIN II
Music by RICHARD RODGERS
Arranged by Phillip Keveren

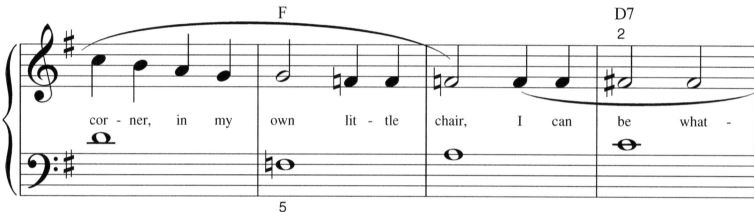

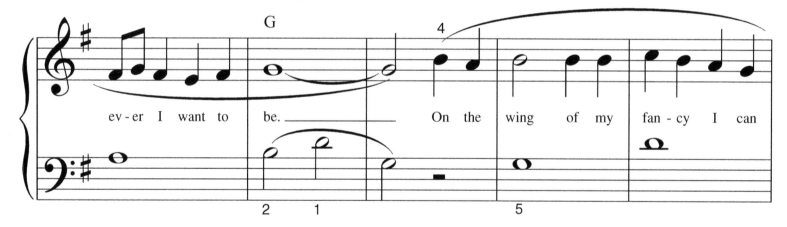

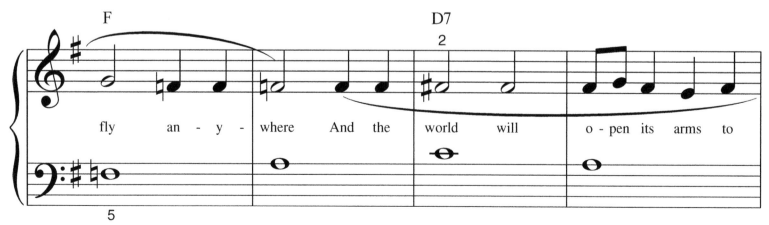

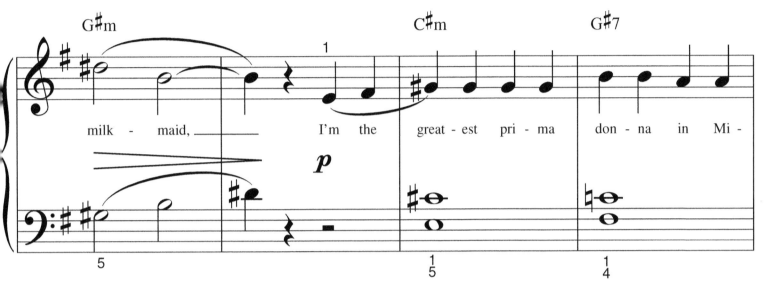

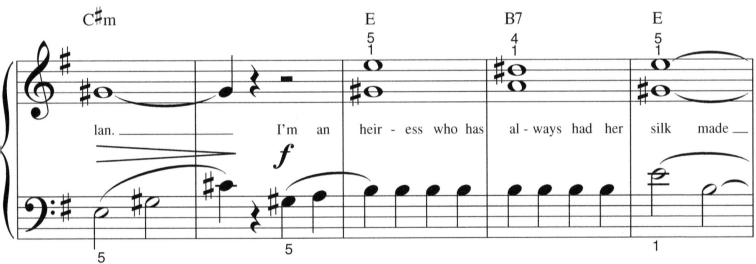

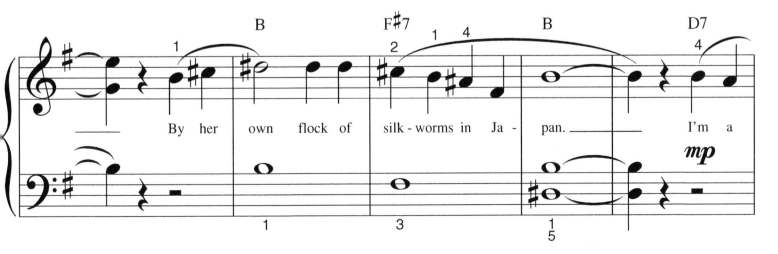

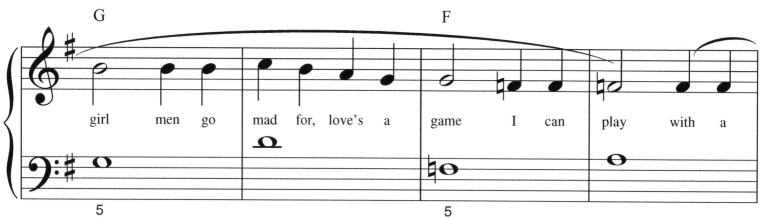

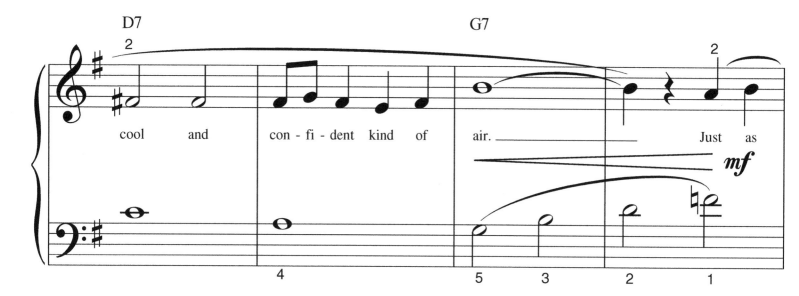

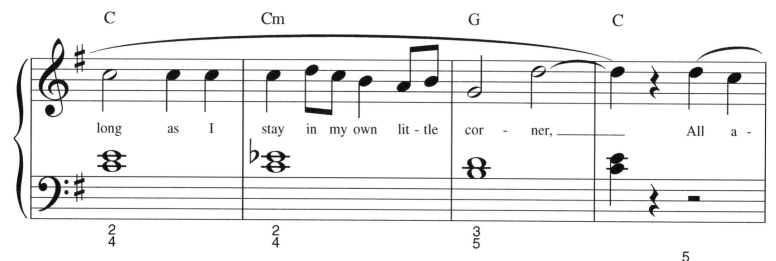

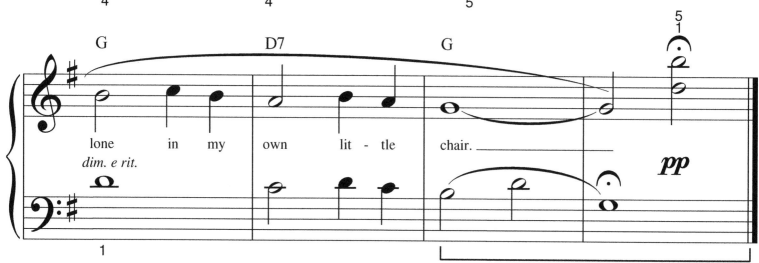

THE RAINBOW CONNECTION

from THE MUPPET MOVIE

Words and Music by PAUL WILLIAMS
and KENNETH L. ASCHER
Arranged by Phillip Keveren

Flowing Waltz

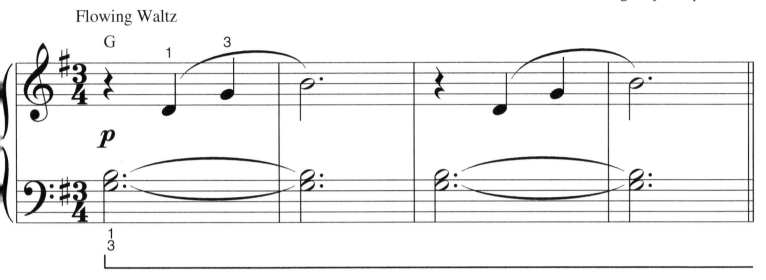

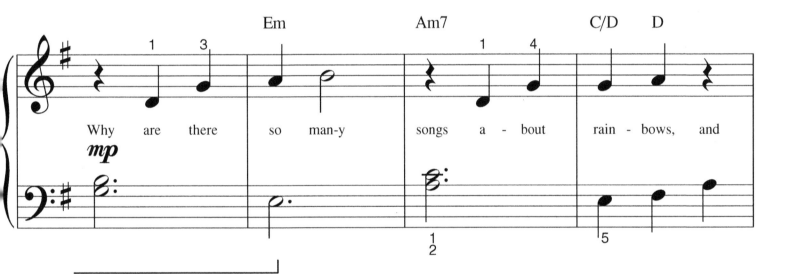

Why are there so man-y songs a-bout rain-bows, and

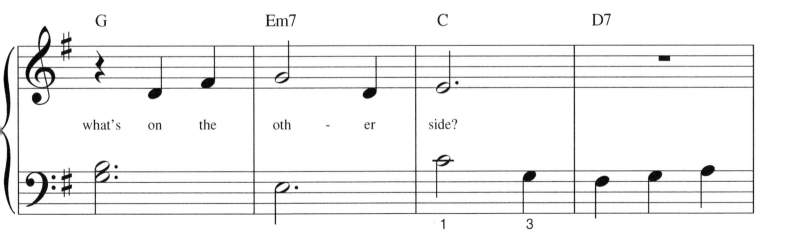

what's on the oth - er side?

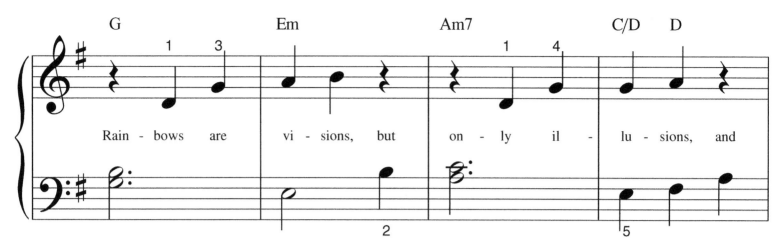

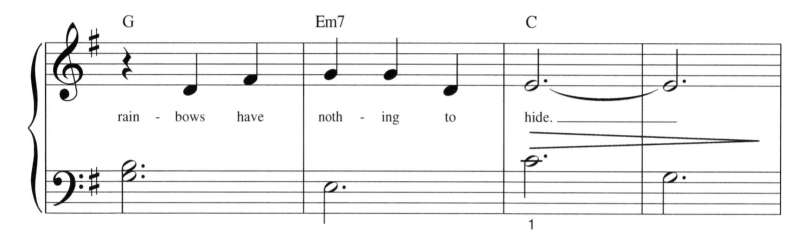

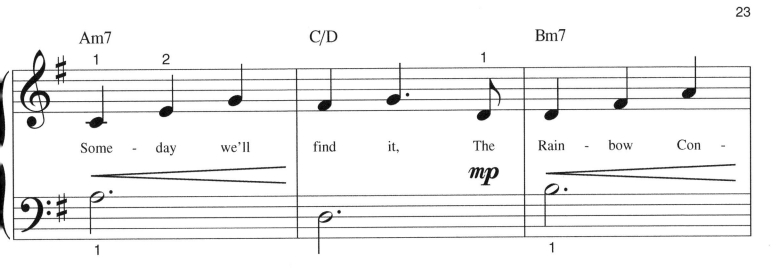

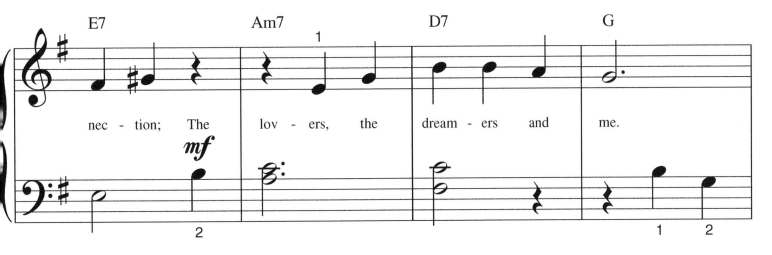

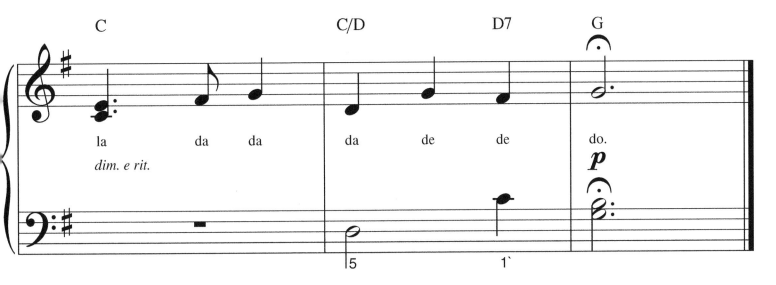

THE LONELY GOATHERD
from THE SOUND OF MUSIC

Lyrics by OSCAR HAMMERSTEIN II
Music by RICHARD RODGERS
Arranged by Phillip Keveren

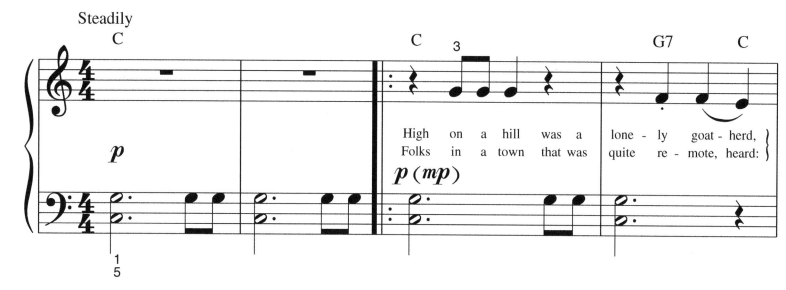

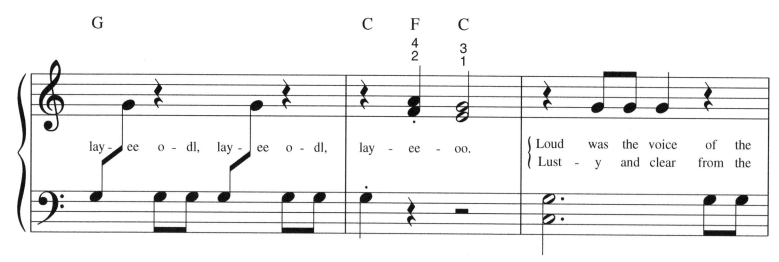

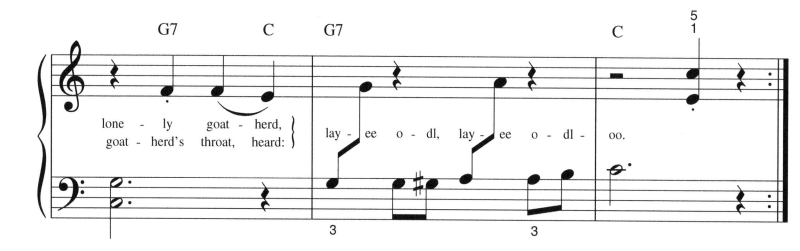

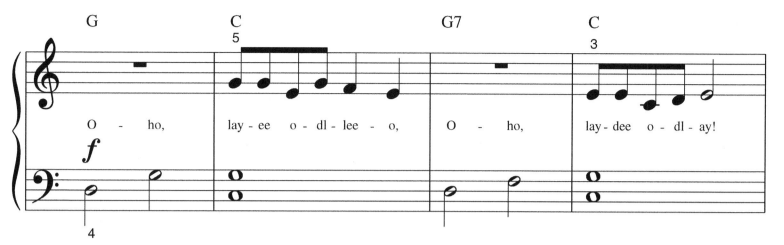

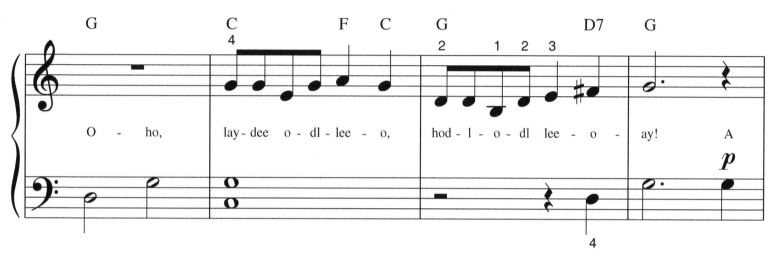

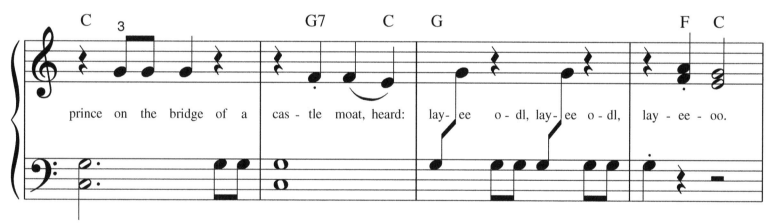

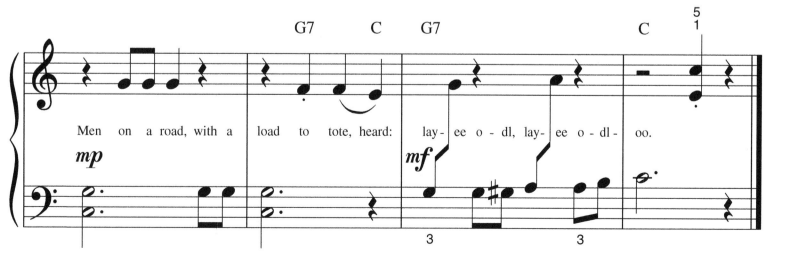

MY FUNNY FRIEND AND ME

from Walt Disney Pictures' THE EMPEROR'S NEW GROOVE

Lyrics by STING
Music by STING and DAVID HARTLEY
Arranged by Phillip Keveren

Warmly

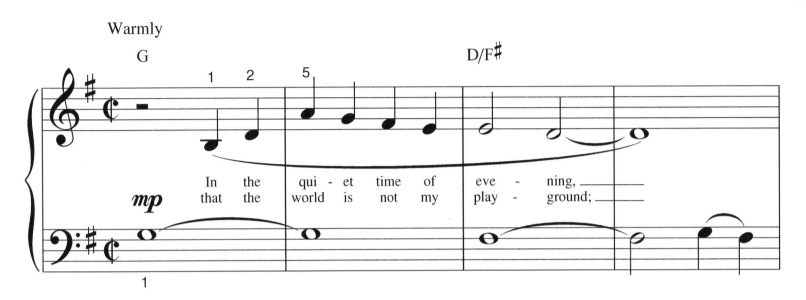

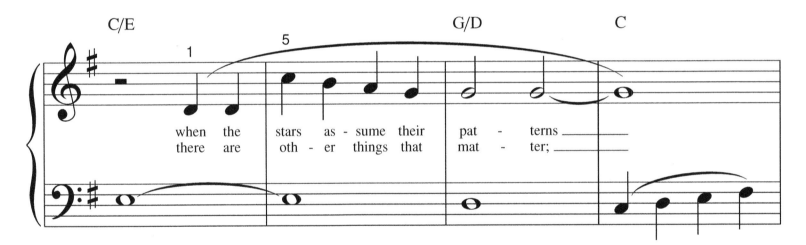

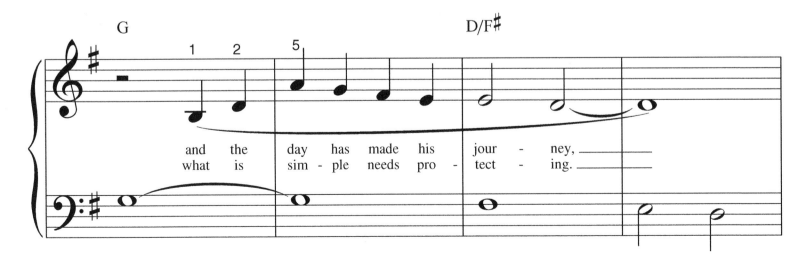

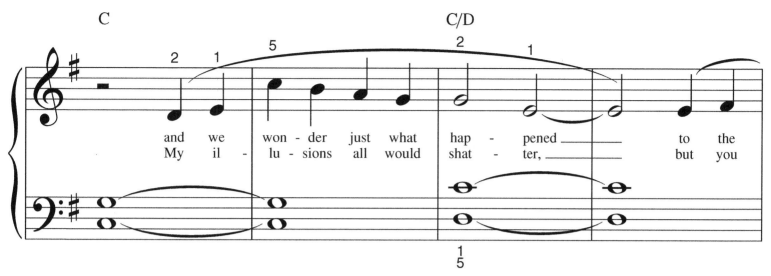

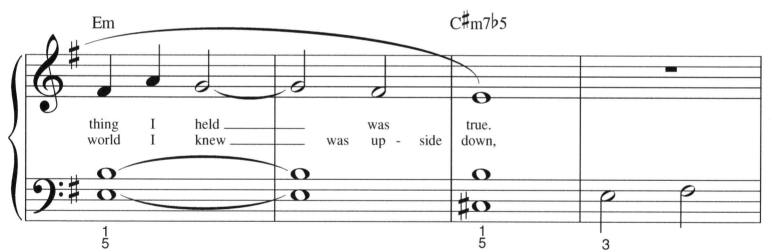

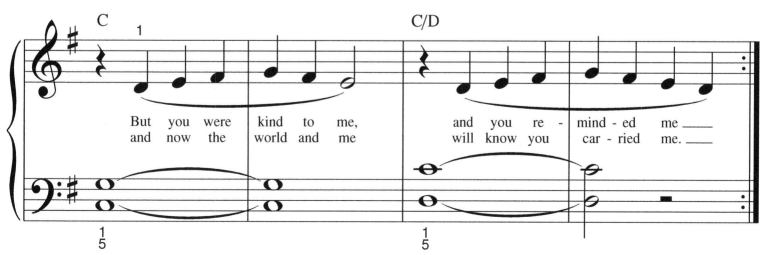

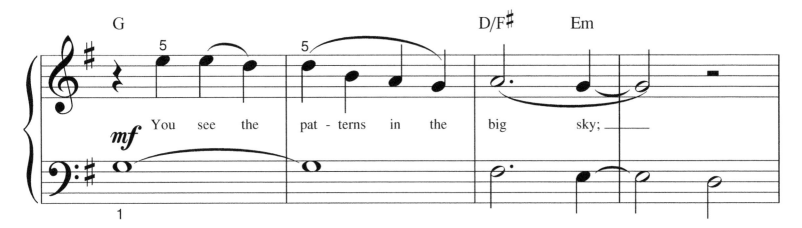

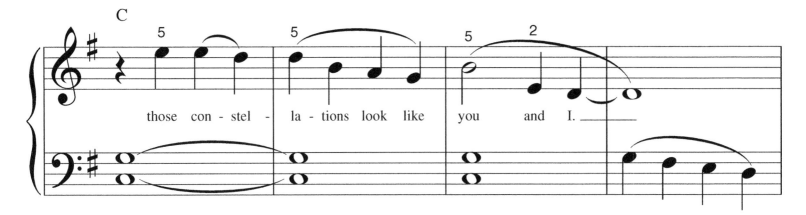

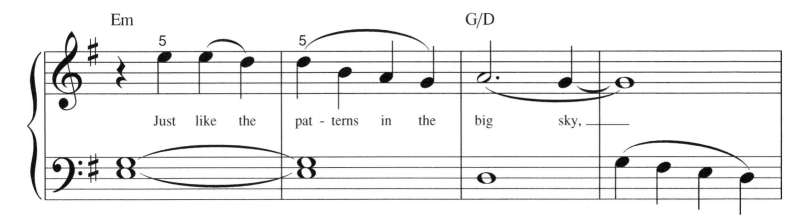

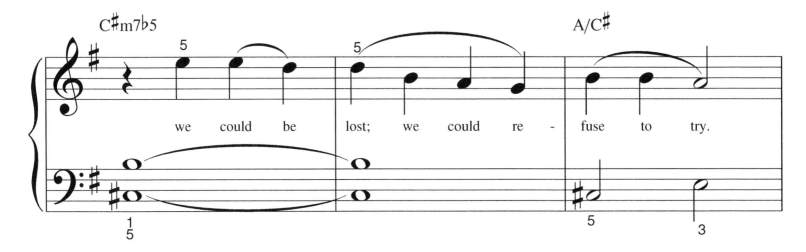

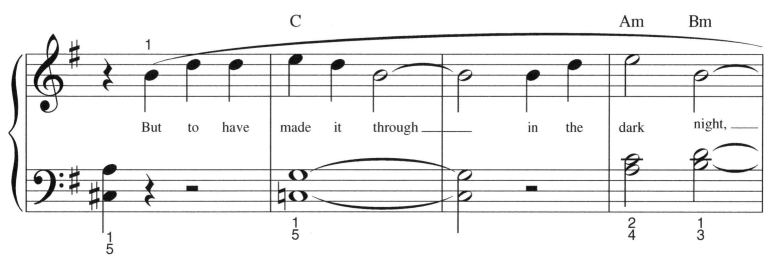

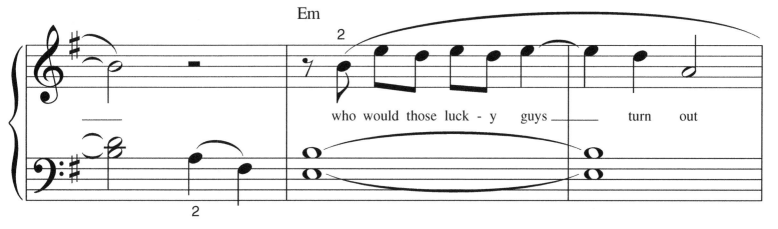

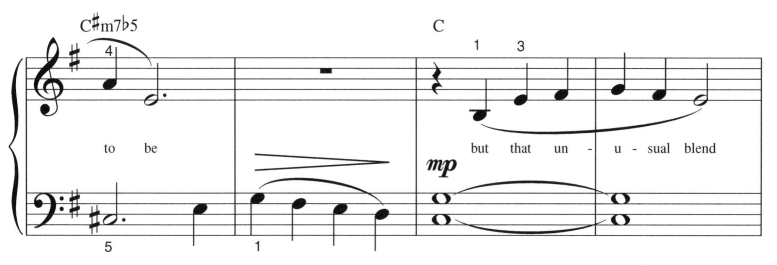

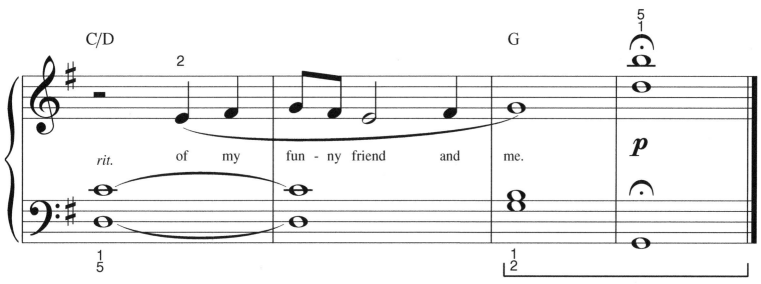

RAIDERS MARCH

from the Paramount Motion Picture RAIDERS OF THE LOST ARK

Music by JOHN WILLIAMS
Arranged by Phillip Keveren

March Tempo

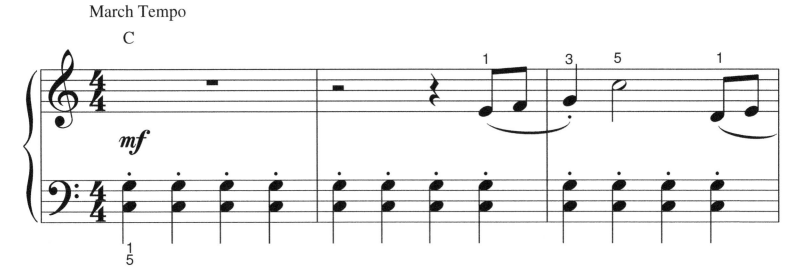

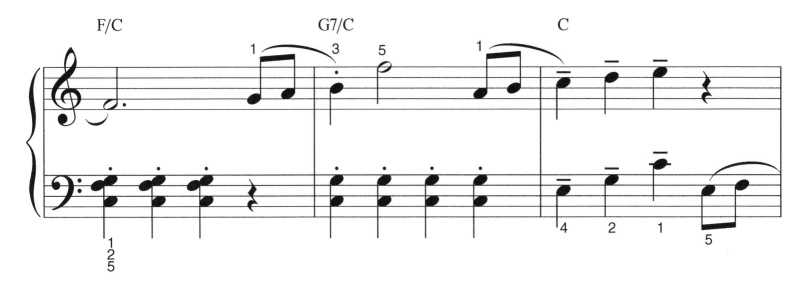

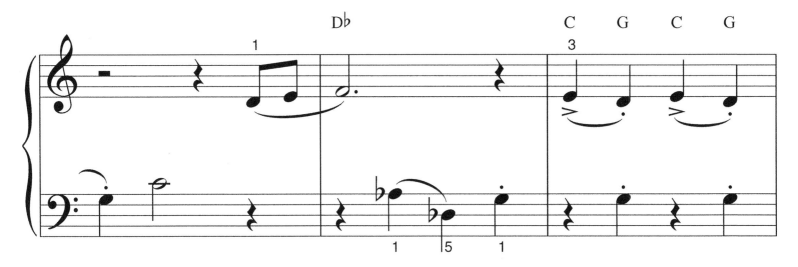

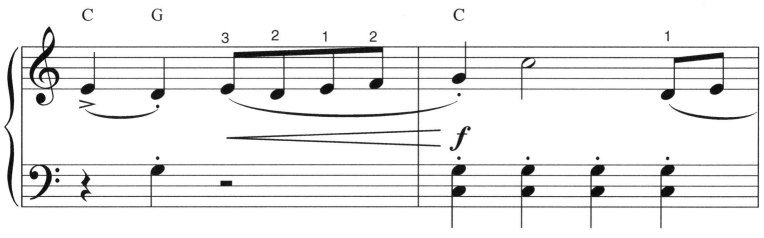
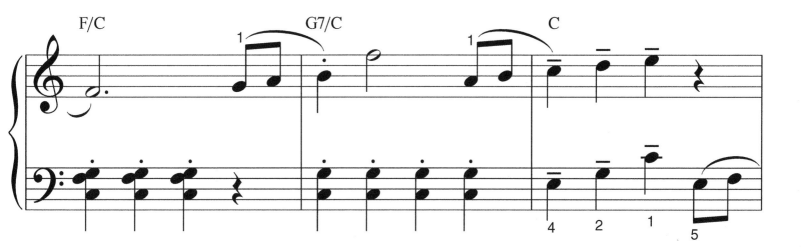
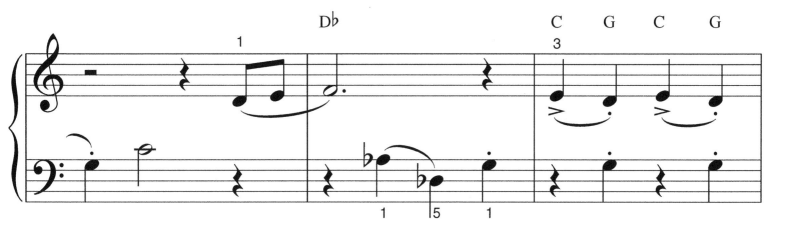
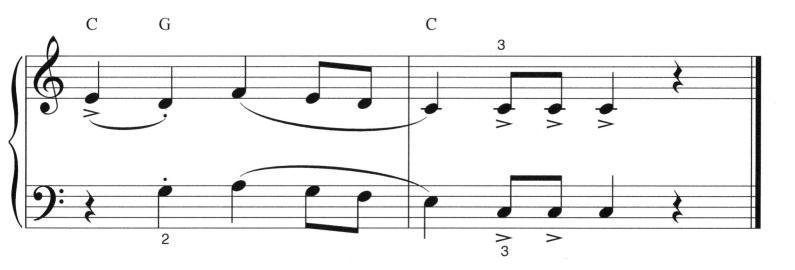

SO LONG, FAREWELL

from THE SOUND OF MUSIC

Lyrics by OSCAR HAMMERSTEIN II
Music by RICHARD RODGERS
Arranged by Phillip Keveren

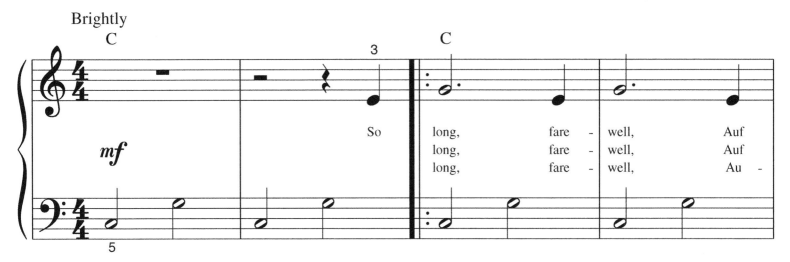

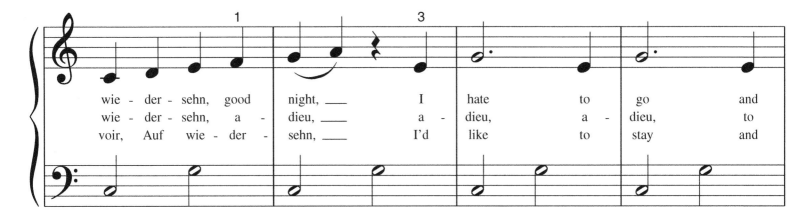

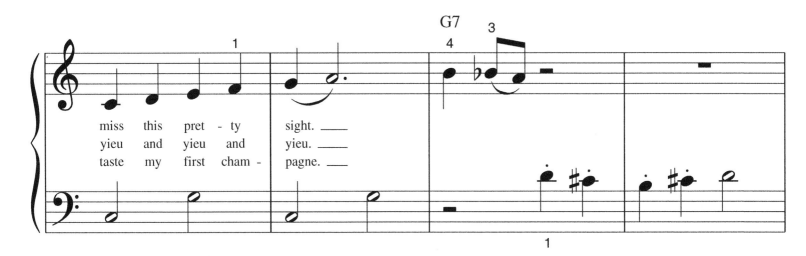

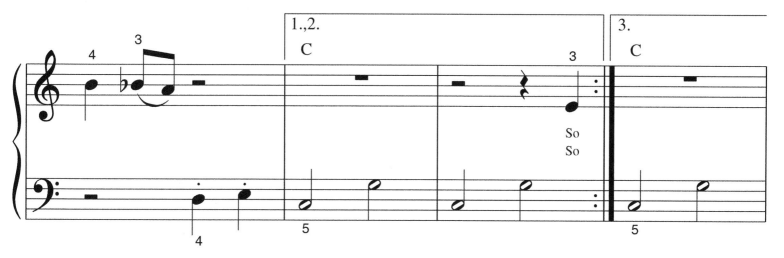

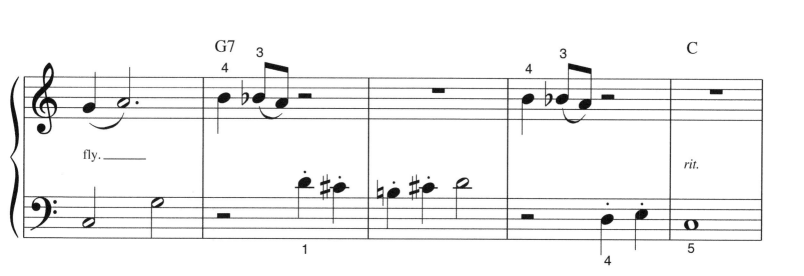

34

Slowly, tranquilly

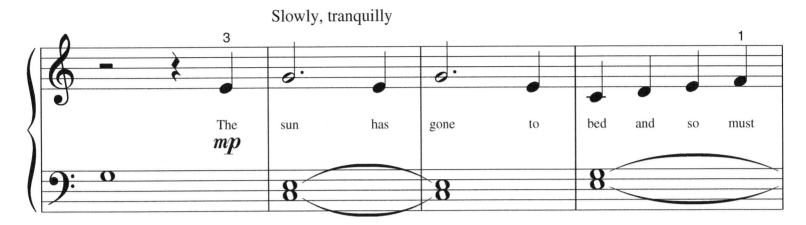

The sun has gone to bed and so must

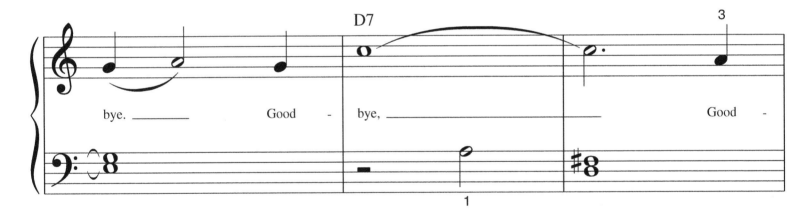

I. _____ So long, fare - well, Auf wie - der - sehn, good -

bye. _____ Good - bye, _____ Good -

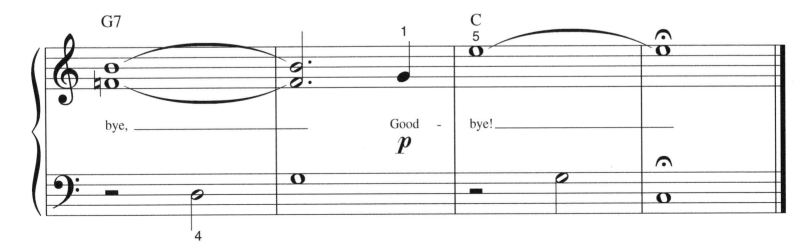

bye, _____ Good - bye! _____

TOMORROW
from the Musical Production ANNIE

Lyric by MARTIN CHARNIN
Music by CHARLES STROUSE
Arranged by Phillip Keveren

Happily

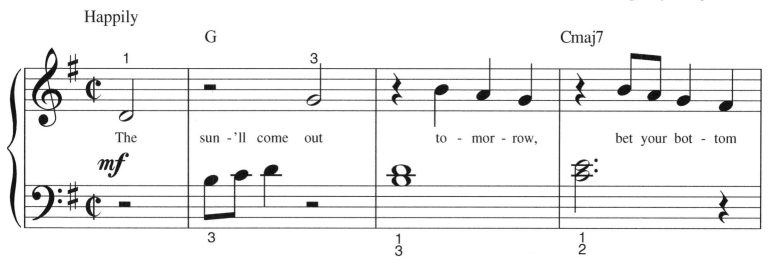

The sun -'ll come out to - mor - row, bet your bot - tom

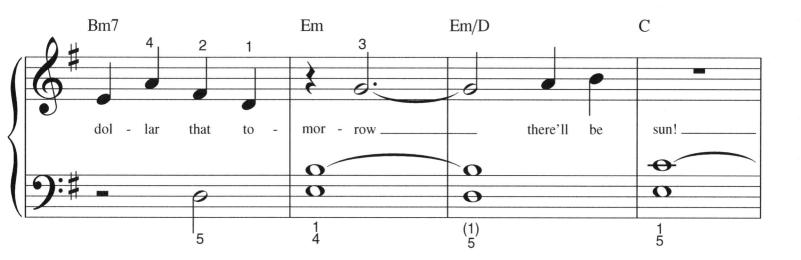

dol - lar that to - mor - row _____ there'll be sun! _____

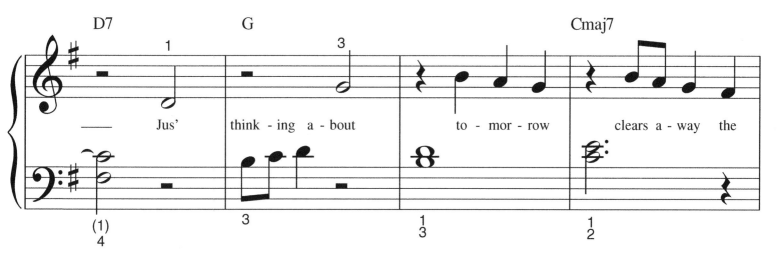

_____ Jus' think - ing a - bout to - mor - row clears a - way the

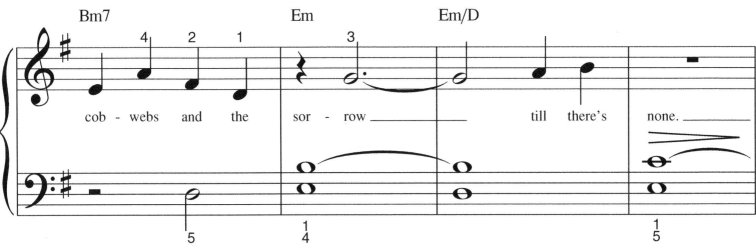

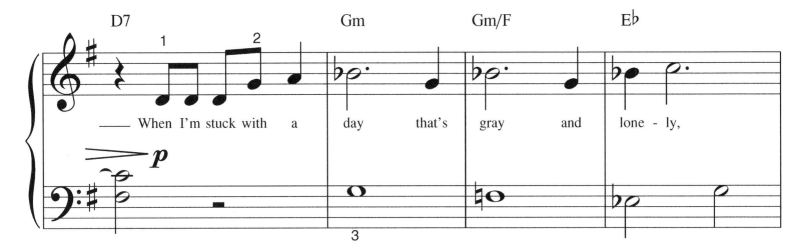

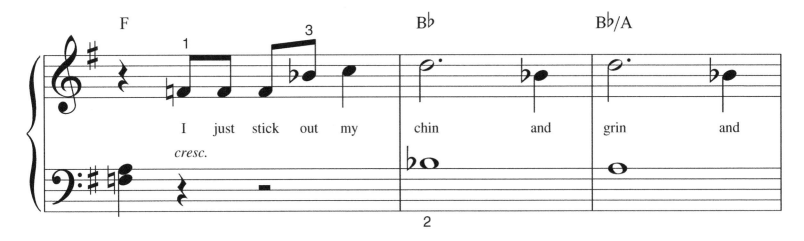

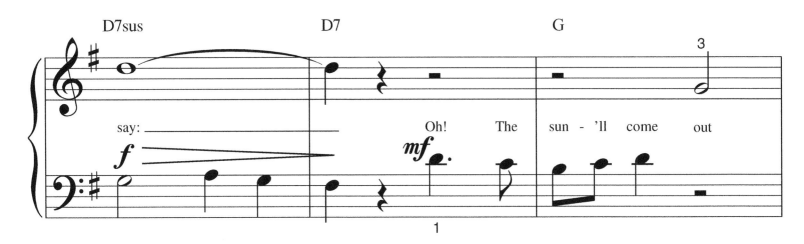

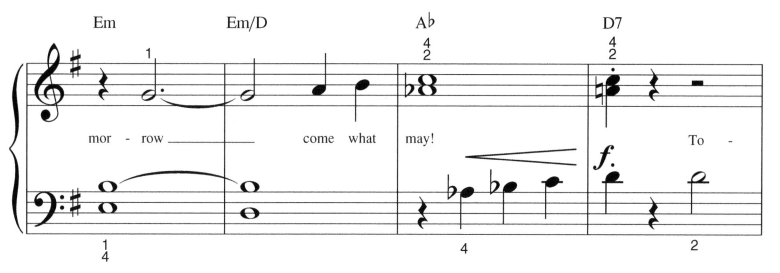

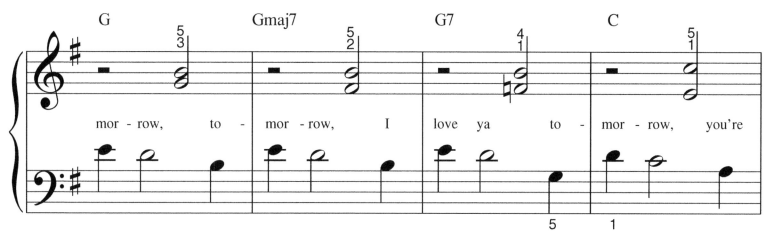

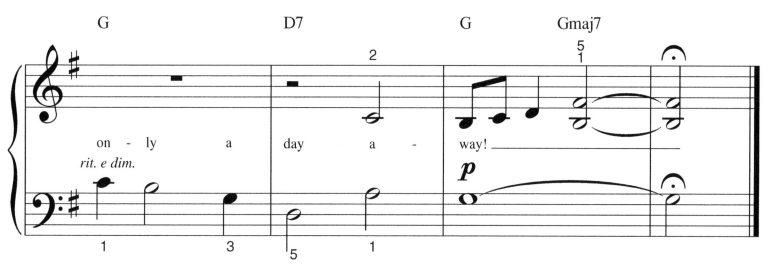

STAR TREK®
THE MOTION PICTURE

Theme from the Paramount Picture STAR TREK: THE MOTION PICTURE

Music by JERRY GOLDSMITH
Arranged by Phillip Keveren

Bright March

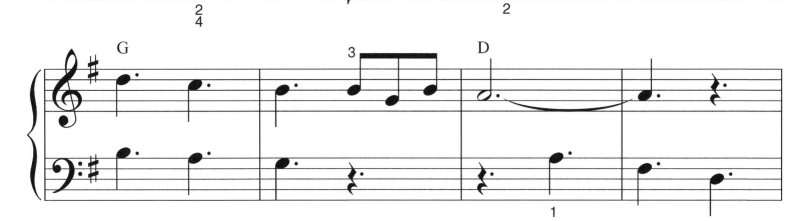

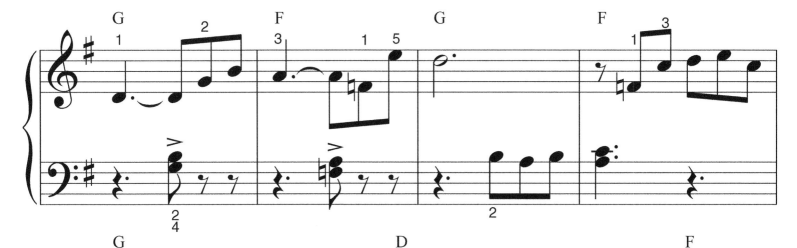

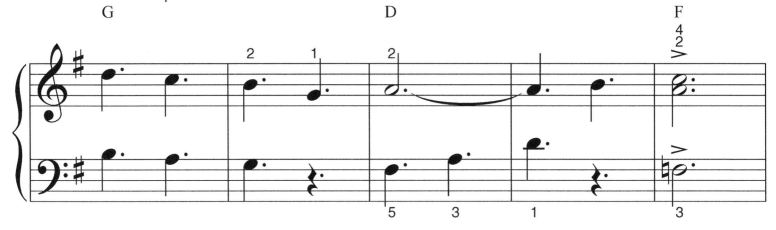

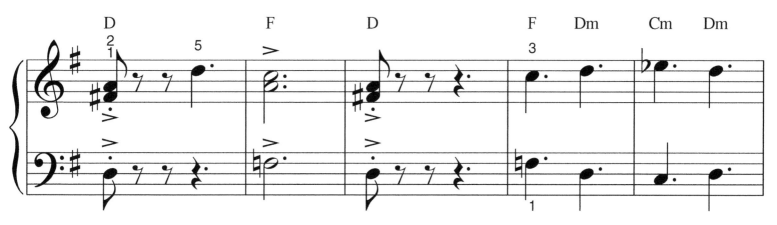

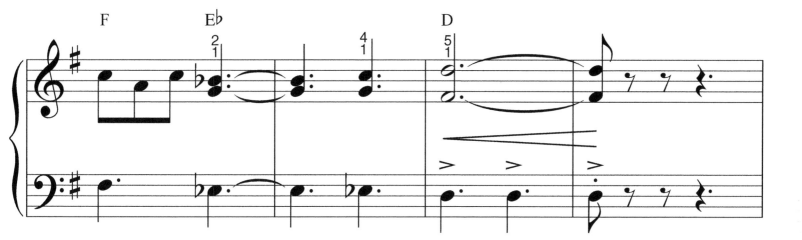

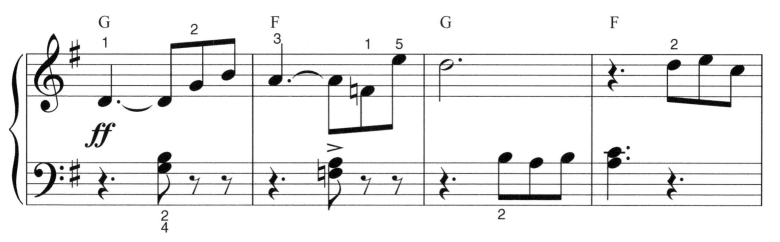

YELLOW SUBMARINE
from YELLOW SUBMARINE

Words and Music by JOHN LENNON
and PAUL McCARTNEY
Arranged by Phillip Keveren

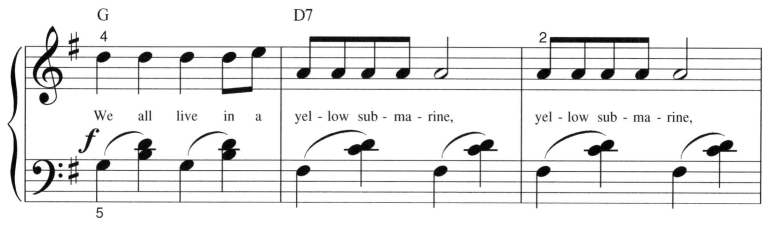

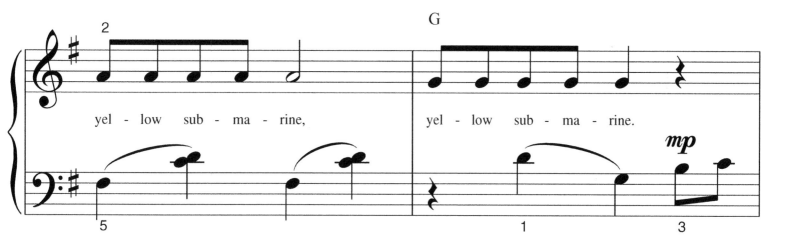

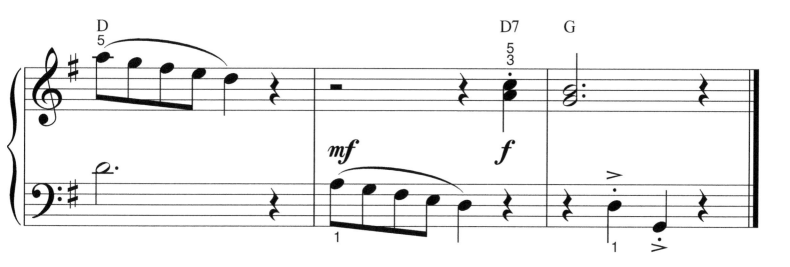

ZIP-A-DEE-DOO-DAH
from Walt Disney's SONG OF THE SOUTH

Words by RAY GILBERT
Music by ALLIE WRUBEL
Arranged by Phillip Keveren

Gleefully

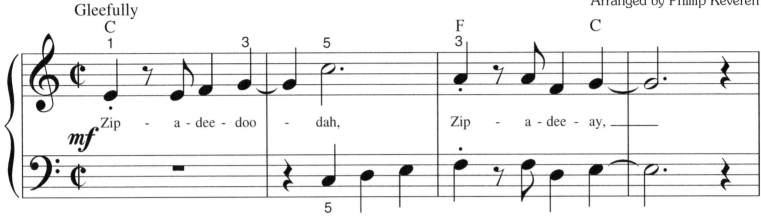

Zip - a-dee-doo - dah, Zip - a-dee-ay,

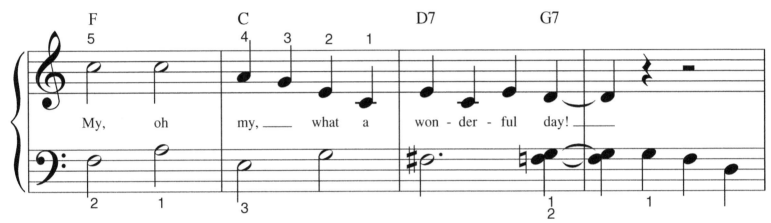

My, oh my, ___ what a won - der - ful day!

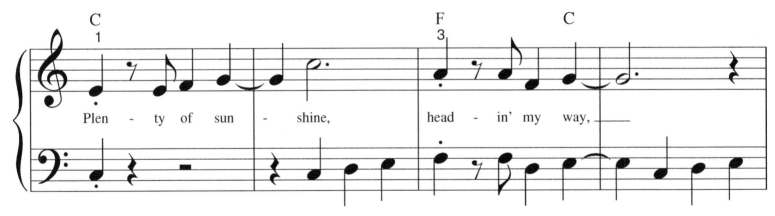

Plen - ty of sun - shine, head - in' my way, ___

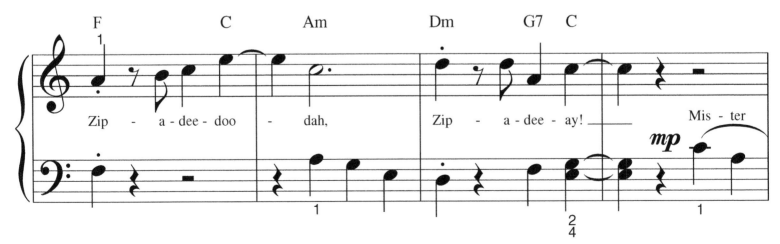

Zip - a-dee-doo - dah, Zip - a-dee-ay! ___ Mis - ter

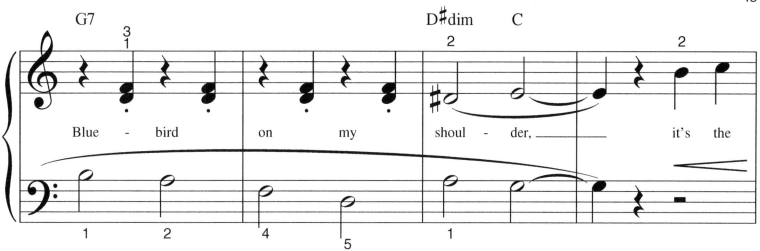

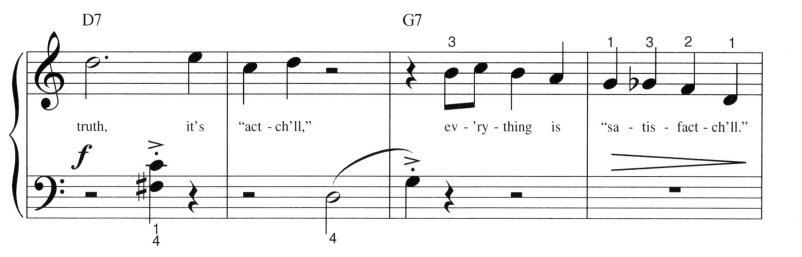

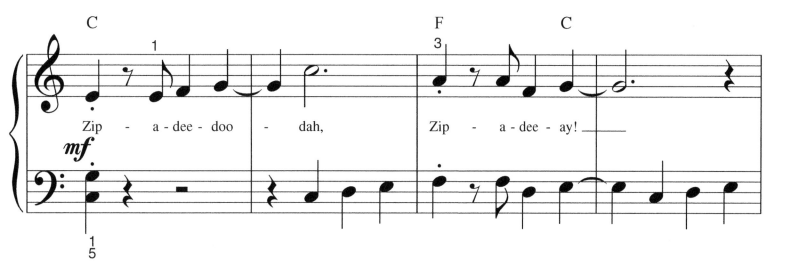

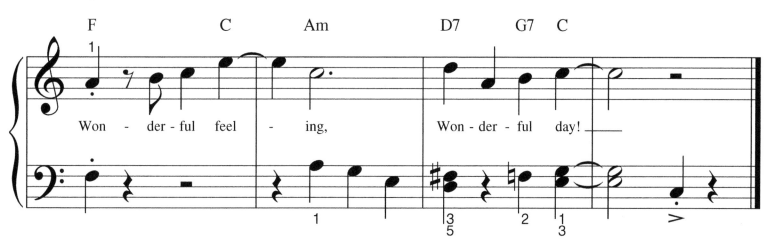

YOU'LL BE IN MY HEART
(Pop Version)
from Walt Disney Pictures' TARZAN™

Words and Music by PHIL COLLINS
Arranged by Phillip Keveren

Come stop your cry - ing; it will be all right.

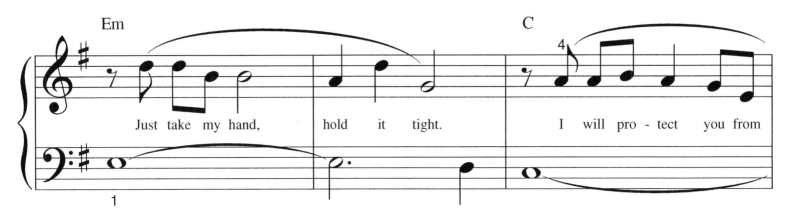

Just take my hand, hold it tight. I will pro - tect you from

all a - round you. I will be here; don't you cry.

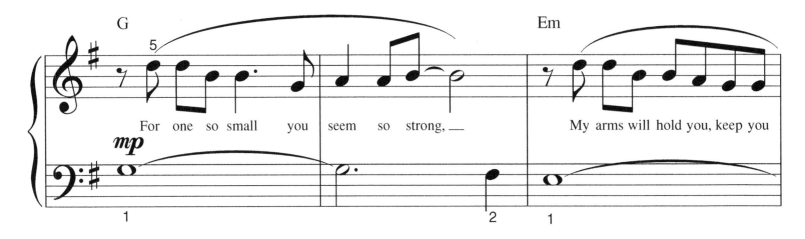

For one so small you seem so strong, My arms will hold you, keep you

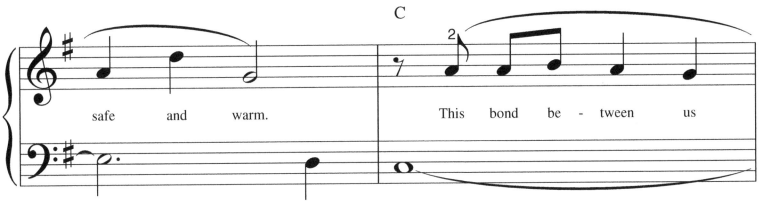

safe and warm. This bond be - tween us

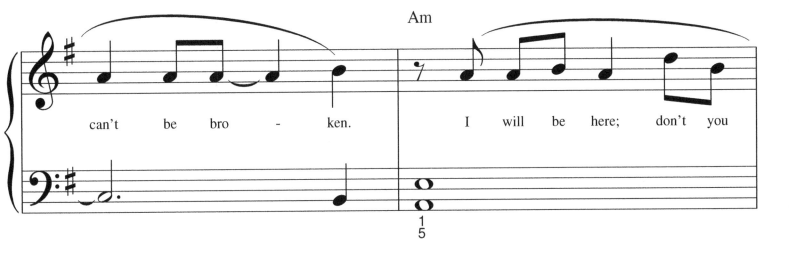

can't be bro - ken. I will be here; don't you

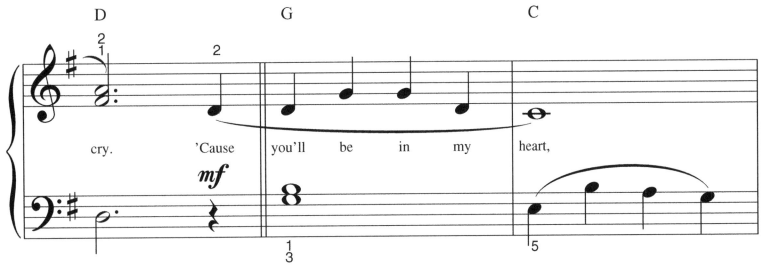

cry. 'Cause you'll be in my heart,

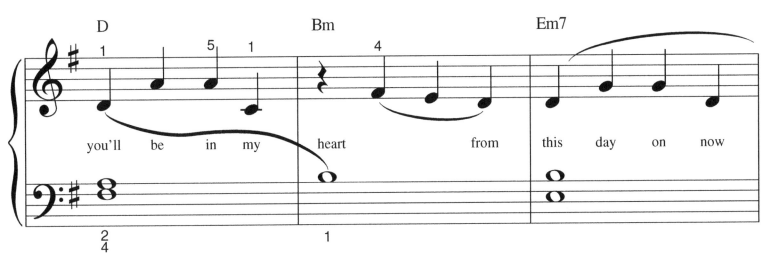

you'll be in my heart from this day on now

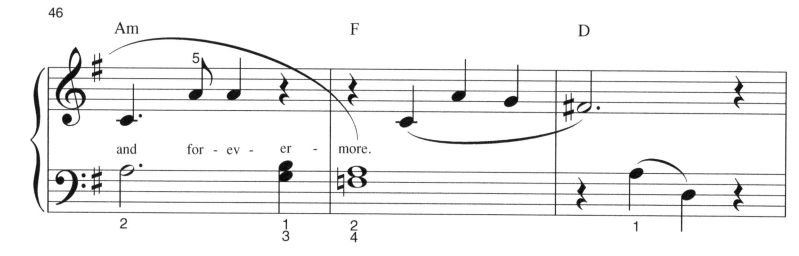

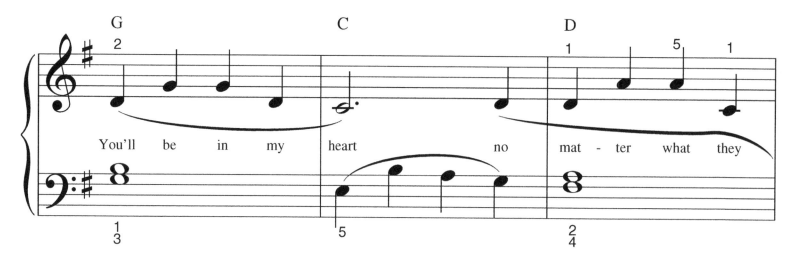

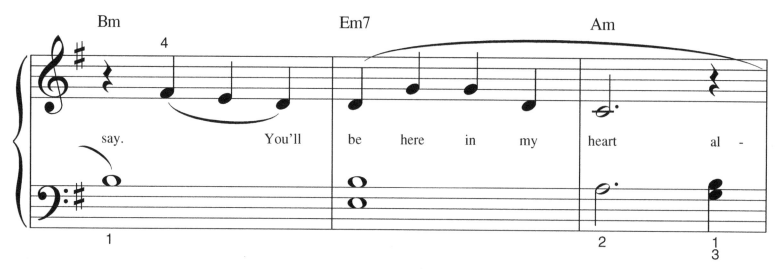

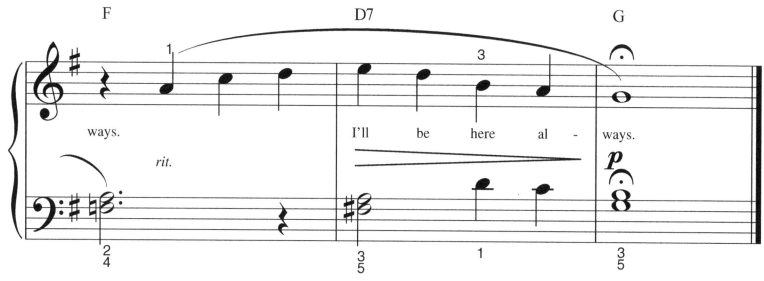

THE PHILLIP KEVEREN SERIES

PIANO SOLO

00156644	**ABBA for Classical Piano**	$15.99
00311024	**Above All**	$12.99
00311348	**Americana**	$12.99
00198473	**Bach Meets Jazz**	$14.99
00313594	**Bacharach and David**	$15.99
00306412	**The Beatles**	$19.99
00312189	**The Beatles for Classical Piano**	$17.99
00275876	**The Beatles – Recital Suites**	$19.99
00312546	**Best Piano Solos**	$15.99
00156601	**Blessings**	$14.99
00198656	**Blues Classics**	$14.99
00284359	**Broadway Songs with a Classical Flair**	$14.99
00310669	**Broadway's Best**	$16.99
00312106	**Canzone Italiana**	$12.99
00280848	**Carpenters**	$17.99
00310629	**A Celtic Christmas**	$14.99
00310549	**The Celtic Collection**	$14.99
00280571	**Celtic Songs with a Classical Flair**	$12.99
00263362	**Charlie Brown Favorites**	$14.99
00312190	**Christmas at the Movies**	$15.99
00294754	**Christmas Carols with a Classical Flair**	$12.99
00311414	**Christmas Medleys**	$14.99
00236669	**Christmas Praise Hymns**	$12.99
00233788	**Christmas Songs for Classical Piano**	$14.99
00311769	**Christmas Worship Medleys**	$14.99
00310607	**Cinema Classics**	$15.99
00301857	**Circles**	$10.99
00311101	**Classic Wedding Songs**	$12.99
00311292	**Classical Folk**	$10.95
00311083	**Classical Jazz**	$14.99
00137779	**Coldplay for Classical Piano**	$16.99
00311103	**Contemporary Wedding Songs**	$12.99
00348788	**Country Songs with a Classical Flair**	$14.99
00249097	**Disney Recital Suites**	$17.99
00311754	**Disney Songs for Classical Piano**	$17.99
00241379	**Disney Songs for Ragtime Piano**	$17.99
00364812	**The Essential Hymn Anthology**	$34.99
00311881	**Favorite Wedding Songs**	$14.99
00315974	**Fiddlin' at the Piano**	$12.99
00311811	**The Film Score Collection**	$15.99
00269408	**Folksongs with a Classical Flair**	$12.99
00144353	**The Gershwin Collection**	$14.99
00233789	**Golden Scores**	$14.99
00144351	**Gospel Greats**	$14.99
00183566	**The Great American Songbook**	$14.99
00312084	**The Great Melodies**	$14.99
00311157	**Great Standards**	$14.99
00171621	**A Grown-Up Christmas List**	$14.99
00311071	**The Hymn Collection**	$14.99
00311349	**Hymn Medleys**	$14.99
00280705	**Hymns in a Celtic Style**	$14.99
00269407	**Hymns with a Classical Flair**	$14.99
00311249	**Hymns with a Touch of Jazz**	$14.99
00310905	**I Could Sing of Your Love Forever**	$16.99
00310762	**Jingle Jazz**	$15.99
00175310	**Billy Joel for Classical Piano**	$16.99
00126449	**Elton John for Classical Piano**	$19.99
00310839	**Let Freedom Ring!**	$12.99
00238988	**Andrew Lloyd Webber Piano Songbook**	$14.99
00313227	**Andrew Lloyd Webber Solos**	$17.99
00313523	**Mancini Magic**	$16.99
00312113	**More Disney Songs for Classical Piano**	$16.99
00311295	**Motown Hits**	$14.99
00300640	**Piano Calm**	$12.99
00339131	**Piano Calm: Christmas**	$14.99
00346009	**Piano Calm: Prayer**	$14.99
00306870	**Piazzolla Tangos**	$17.99
00386709	**Praise and Worship for Classical Piano**	$14.99
00156645	**Queen for Classical Piano**	$17.99
00310755	**Richard Rodgers Classics**	$17.99
00289545	**Scottish Songs**	$12.99
00119403	**The Sound of Music**	$16.99
00311978	**The Spirituals Collection**	$12.99
00366023	**So Far...**	$14.99
00210445	**Star Wars**	$16.99
00224738	**Symphonic Hymns for Piano**	$14.99
00366022	**Three-Minute Encores**	$16.99
00279673	**Tin Pan Alley**	$12.99
00312112	**Treasured Hymns for Classical Piano**	$15.99
00144926	**The Twelve Keys of Christmas**	$14.99
00278486	**The Who for Classical Piano**	$16.99
00294036	**Worship with a Touch of Jazz**	$14.99
00311911	**Yuletide Jazz**	$19.99

EASY PIANO

00210401	**Adele for Easy Classical Piano**	$17.99
00310610	**African-American Spirituals**	$12.99
00218244	**The Beatles for Easy Classical Piano**	$14.99
00218387	**Catchy Songs for Piano**	$12.99
00310973	**Celtic Dreams**	$12.99
00233686	**Christmas Carols for Easy Classical Piano**	$14.99
00311126	**Christmas Pops**	$16.99
00368199	**Christmas Reflections**	$14.99
00311548	**Classic Pop/Rock Hits**	$14.99
00310769	**A Classical Christmas**	$14.99
00310975	**Classical Movie Themes**	$12.99
00144352	**Disney Songs for Easy Classical Piano**	$14.99
00311093	**Early Rock 'n' Roll**	$14.99
00311997	**Easy Worship Medleys**	$14.99
00289547	**Duke Ellington**	$14.99
00160297	**Folksongs for Easy Classical Piano**	$12.99

00110374	**George Gershwin Classics**	$14.99
00310805	**Gospel Treasures**	$14.99
00306821	**Vince Guaraldi Collection**	$19.99
00160294	**Hymns for Easy Classical Piano**	$14.99
00310798	**Immortal Hymns**	$12.99
00311294	**Jazz Standards**	$12.99
00355474	**Living Hope**	$14.99
00310744	**Love Songs**	$14.99
00233740	**The Most Beautiful Songs for Easy Classical Piano**	$12.99
00220036	**Pop Ballads**	$14.99
00311406	**Pop Gems of the 1950s**	$12.95
00233739	**Pop Standards for Easy Classical Piano**	$12.99
00102887	**A Ragtime Christmas**	$12.99
00311293	**Ragtime Classics**	$14.99
00312028	**Santa Swings**	$14.99
00233688	**Songs from Childhood for Easy Classical Piano**	$12.99
00103258	**Songs of Inspiration**	$14.99
00310840	**Sweet Land of Liberty**	$12.99
00126450	**10,000 Reasons**	$16.99
00310712	**Timeless Praise**	$14.99
00311086	**TV Themes**	$14.99
00310717	**21 Great Classics**	$14.99
00160076	**Waltzes & Polkas for Easy Classical Piano**	$12.99
00145342	**Weekly Worship**	$17.99

BIG-NOTE PIANO

00310838	**Children's Favorite Movie Songs**	$14.99
00346000	**Christmas Movie Magic**	$12.99
00277368	**Classical Favorites**	$12.99
00277370	**Disney Favorites**	$14.99
00310888	**Joy to the World**	$12.99
00310908	**The Nutcracker**	$12.99
00277371	**Star Wars**	$16.99

BEGINNING PIANO SOLOS

00311202	**Awesome God**	$14.99
00310837	**Christian Children's Favorites**	$14.99
00311117	**Christmas Traditions**	$10.99
00311250	**Easy Hymns**	$12.99
00102710	**Everlasting God**	$10.99
00311403	**Jazzy Tunes**	$10.95
00310822	**Kids' Favorites**	$12.99
00367778	**A Magical Christmas**	$14.99
00338175	**Silly Songs for Kids**	$9.99

PIANO DUET

00126452	**The Christmas Variations**	$14.99
00362562	**Classic Piano Duets**	$14.99
00311350	**Classical Theme Duets**	$12.99
00295099	**Gospel Duets**	$12.99
00311544	**Hymn Duets**	$14.99
00311203	**Praise & Worship Duets**	$14.99
00294755	**Sacred Christmas Duets**	$14.99
00119405	**Star Wars**	$16.99
00253545	**Worship Songs for Two**	$12.99

Big Fun with Big-Note Piano Books!

These songbooks feature exciting easy arrangements for beginning piano students.

Beatles' Best
27 classics for beginners to enjoy, including: Can't Buy Me Love • Eleanor Rigby • Hey Jude • Michelle • Here, There and Everywhere • When I'm Sixty-Four • Yesterday • and more.
00222561...$17.99

The Best Songs Ever
70 favorites, featuring: Body and Soul • Crazy • Edelweiss • Fly Me to the Moon • Georgia on My Mind • Imagine • The Lady Is a Tramp • Memory • A String of Pearls • Tears in Heaven • Unforgettable • You Are So Beautiful • and more.
00310425...$24.99

Chart Hits of 2020-2021
16 of the top hits of 2020 into 2021, including: Drivers License (Olivia Rodrigo) • Dynamite (BTS) • Kings & Queens (Ava Max) • Positions (Ariana Grande) • Therefore I Am (Billie Eilish) • Watermelon Sugar (Harry Styles) • Willow (Taylor Swift) • and more.
00364362...$16.99

Children's Favorite Movie Songs
arranged by Phillip Keveren
16 favorites from films, including: The Bare Necessities • Beauty and the Beast • Can You Feel the Love Tonight • Do-Re-Mi • The Rainbow Connection • Tomorrow • Zip-A-Dee-Doo-Dah • and more.
00310838...$14.99

Disney Big-Note Collection
Over 40 Disney favorites, including: Circle of Life • Colors of the Wind • Hakuna Matata • It's a Small World • Under the Sea • A Whole New World • Winnie the Pooh • Zip-A-Dee-Doo-Dah • and more.
00316056...$22.99

Favorite Children's Songs
arranged by Bill Boyd
29 easy arrangements of songs to play and sing with children: Peter Cottontail • I Whistle a Happy Tune • It's a Small World • On the Good Ship Lollipop • The Rainbow Connection • and more!
00240251...$14.99

Favorite TV Themes
22 themes from the small screen, including: Addams Family Theme • Happy Days • Jeopardy Theme • Mission: Impossible Theme • Price Is Right (Opening Theme) • Sesame Street Theme • Won't You Be My Neighbor? • and more.
00294318...$10.99

Frozen
9 songs from this hit Disney film, plus full-color illustrations from the movie. Songs include the standout single "Let It Go", plus: Do You Want to Build a Snowman? • For the First Time in Forever • Reindeer(s) Are Better Than People • and more.
00126105...$15.99

The Great Big Book of Children's Songs – 2nd Edition
66 super tunes that kids adore, includes: Circle of Life • Edelweiss • If I Only Had a Brain • Over the Rainbow • Puff the Magic Dragon • Rubber Duckie • Sing • This Land Is Your Land • Under the Sea • and dozens more!
00119364...$17.99

Happy Birthday to You and Other Great Songs for Big-Note Piano
16 essential favorites, including: Chitty Chitty Bang Bang • Good Night • Happy Birthday to You • Heart and Soul • Over the Rainbow • Sing • This Land Is Your Land • and more.
00119636...$9.99

Modern Movie Favorites
Beginning pianists will love to play the 18 familiar movie hits in this collection, including: The Bare Necessities • Can't Stop the Feeling • City of Stars • How Far I'll Go • In Summer • Rey's Theme • Something Wild • and more.
00241880...$14.99

Pride & Prejudice
Music from the Motion Picture Soundtrack
12 piano pieces from the 2006 Oscar-nominated film: Another Dance • Darcy's Letter • Georgiana • Leaving Netherfield • Liz on Top of the World • Meryton Townhall • The Secret Life of Daydreams • Stars and Butterflies • and more.
00316125...$16.99

Songs of Peace, Hope and Love
30 inspirational and motivational songs, including: Bridge over Troubled Water • The Climb • Hallelujah • Over the Rainbow • Put a Little Love in Your Heart • What a Wonderful World • You Raise Me Up • and more.
00119634...$12.99

Star Wars
13 Selections from a Galaxy Far, Far Away
A baker's dozen of Star Wars selections by John Williams arranged by Phillip Keveren, include: Across the Stars (Love Theme from Star Wars) • The Imperial March (Darth Vader's Theme) • Luke and Leia • Rey's Theme • Star Wars (Main Theme) • and more.
00277371...$17.99

Today's Pop Hits – 3rd Edition
A great collection of current pop hits that even developing piano players will be able to enjoy. 15 songs with lyrics, including: All of Me • Happy • Hello • Pompeii • Radioactive • Roar • Shake It Off • Stay with Me • Story of My Life • and more.
00160577 ....$16.99

Top Hits of 2019
17 of the year's best are included in this collection for easy to read big note piano with lyrics: Gloria • I Don't Care • Lo/Hi • ME! • Old Town Road (Remix) • Senorita • Someone You Loved • Sucker • and more.
00302427...$14.99

The Big-Note Worship Book – 2nd Edition
20 selections for budding pianists looking to play their favorite worship songs: Everlasting God • Holy Is the Lord • In Christ Alone • Revelation Song • 10,000 Reasons (Bless the Lord) • Your Grace Is Enough • and more.
00267812...$14.99

HAL•LEONARD®
Complete song lists online at
www.halleonard.com